HOW TO CANCEL AMAZON AUDIBLE SUBSCRIPTION

A QUICK GUIDE

Copyright

All rights reserved. No part of this publication may be reproduced, distributed, or transmitted in any form or by any means, including photocopying, recording, or other electronic or mechanical methods, without the prior written permission of the publisher, except in the case of brief quotations embodied in critical reviews and certain other non-commercial uses permitted by copyright law.

BlazeTech, 2024, all rights reserved.

Table of Content

Copyright 1
Table of Content 2
INTRODUCTION 4
Chapter 1 14
    What Is Audible? 14
        Key Features 14
        Subscription Benefits 26
Chapter 2 37
    Reasons to Cancel Audible 37
        Common Issues with Audible 37
        Changing Preferences and Alternative Options 42
Chapter 3 47
    Canceling Your Audible Subscription 47
        Step-by-Step Instructions: 47
        Troubleshooting Tips: 52
Chapter 4 59
    Addressing Attachment When Cancelling Audible 59
        Recognize emotional attachment: 59
        Reflect on Reasons for Attachment: 60
        Embrace change and Growth: 62
Conclusion 64

If you find this book helpful at the end, we would be deeply grateful if you could take a moment to leave a positive and honest review. Your feedback is incredibly important.

Warmest regards,
BlazeTech

INTRODUCTION

In particular, if you have been used to the ease and extensive range of audiobooks that Audible offers, canceling your membership to Amazon Audible may seem like a daunting commitment. However, there are a lot of other reasons why you could think about making this adjustment. You could discover that the titles you desire are not available, or that the cost of the membership no longer falls within your financial means. It's possible that your preferences for various sorts of entertainment have changed and that you now prefer listening to other types of media. It is possible that your selection will also be influenced by technical challenges as well as a lack of adequate customer assistance.

The accessibility of literature and information that audiobooks provide is something that conventional reading may not always be able to provide. Audiobooks have become an essential component of our lives. Individuals who have issues reading or who have visual impairments are able to appreciate books, and they also enable the freedom to listen while doing many tasks at the same time. In addition to the fact that there are a wide variety of genres accessible, the improved experience that comes with professional narrations brings a new and distinctive facet to the art of storytelling.

It is essential to be able to identify when a service no longer satisfies your requirements, despite the fact that Audible provides services that are beneficial. When you switch from Audible to another audiobook service, it does not mean that you are giving up on the pleasure of listening to audiobooks; rather, it simply indicates that you are looking for a service that is a better match for your current lifestyle and interests. Your Audible membership may be terminated and alternative audiobook possibilities can be investigated with the help of this book, which will provide you with detailed, step-by-step instructions on how to do so.

It is necessary to have a solid understanding of the primary features and advantages of Audible in order to fully understand the reasons why you may have first selected it. Due to its huge collection, user-friendly layout, and high-quality audio recording, Audible has become an indispensable resource for a large number of people who like listening to audiobooks. The service claims to provide simplicity and really delivers on that promise, with features such as synchronization that is smooth across all devices and tailored suggestions. It is possible to have a better understanding of the reasons for your consideration of a change by first acknowledging the usual problems that consumers encounter, such as the cost, the availability of content, and technological challenges. To provide you with a full grasp of the possible negatives and growing requirements that may inspire your choice, we will dig into these factors in depth and provide extensive information.

One of the most important considerations for many customers is the cost. In particular, if you are not making as much use of the service as you had planned, the monthly costs for Audible may quickly pile up. When monthly credits are not utilized, it might give the impression that money has been wasted. In addition, some customers discover that even with a subscription, the cost of buying extra audiobooks that are not included in the monthly credits might be exorbitant. In many cases, the decision to terminate the service is made due to the financial concerns that are being taken into account.

An additional crucial concern is the accessibility of the content. While Audible has a large collection, it is not thorough in its selection of books. The frustration that might result from the fact that you regularly find yourself looking for books that are not accessible on Audible is a common occurrence. If you are seeking non-English titles, independent writers, or niche genres that Audible may not highlight in its collection, then this dissatisfaction will be amplified for you. The service's usefulness decreases when the material that you wish to access is not easily accessible.

There is also the possibility that technical glitches may detract from the overall experience. It is not impossible for Audible to have faults and malfunctions, despite the fact that its interface is normally easy to use. Inconveniences of a severe kind include the app crashing, problems with synchronizing across devices, and unsuccessful downloads. It is possible that these problems will have a major effect on your enjoyment of the service if they continue to exist and are not fixed.

Many people fail to take into account the emotional journey that comes with terminating a subscription service. A mixture of melancholy and trepidation is perfectly natural, but this is also a time to investigate new avenues of possibility. Many people consider Audible to be more than simply a service; it is a companion that they may use throughout their commutes, workouts, or quiet times at home. Canceling a reservation might seem like parting ways with a reliable companion. Having said that, it is of the utmost importance to keep in mind that the purpose of this option is to significantly improve your entire experience. We will address these aspects of your mental state, providing you with comfort and support in order to assist you in feeling secure in your choice.

We will look at the features and offers of several alternative audiobook services as we investigate them, with the goal of assisting you in making an educated decision. There is a wide variety of choices accessible, each of which comes with its own set of benefits. For example, sites such as Scribd provide a subscription model that allows users to have unrestricted access to a variety of material, including audiobooks, e-books, and other forms of media. Libby is one of the many services that provide free access to audiobooks via your local library. Each of the available options comes with its own individual set of characteristics, advantages, and drawbacks. Through the examination of these choices, you will be able to locate a service that is more suitable to your requirements and tastes.

To ensure a seamless transition to a new service, it is necessary to take actionable measures and follow some helpful guidelines in order to locate new audiobooks and effectively manage the move. This book will provide you with the information and skills you need to make this shift as smooth and unobtrusive as possible. The process of switching providers does not have to be one that induces disruption. If you get the appropriate direction, you will have no trouble transferring your library, finding new material, and adjusting to a different platform. We are going to go over everything, from registering for a new provider to moving your audiobooks and becoming acclimated to a new user interface.

In order to get the most out of your audiobook experience without using Audible, you should investigate free resources and libraries. This will ensure that you continue to have access to a wide variety of audiobooks as you listen to them. Through applications like Libby and Hoopla, public libraries, for example, provide access to a vast collection of audiobooks that are available at no cost. When it comes to passionate listeners who are on a budget, these tools might be really helpful.

In addition, there are a lot of websites that provide free audiobooks, especially for works that are considered to be in the public domain. We will provide you with hints and suggestions to improve your listening experience and make the most of the many choices that are accessible to you.

To summarize, terminating your membership to Audible is a serious choice; but, it does not have to be a difficult one. With this book, you will be able to make the most informed decision possible on your audiobook requirements, as it will provide you with clarity and assistance during each stage of the process. This is the place where you will get the knowledge and confidence that you need, regardless of whether you are motivated by concerns about costs, shifting preferences, or a desire to investigate new possibilities. By terminating your membership, you are not only releasing yourself from a subscription, but you are also releasing yourself to new and exciting possibilities in the world of audiobooks.

Keep in mind that the objective is to improve the quality of your audiobook experience by locating the appropriate service that is suitable for your lifestyle and the requirements you already have. Now, give yourself a moment to relax and take a big breath before we go off on this adventure together. By terminating your membership, you are not only releasing yourself from a subscription, but you are also releasing yourself to new and exciting possibilities in the world of audiobooks. In order to ensure that your passion for audiobooks continues to develop and bloom in the most optimal manner, this journey is all about finding the correct match for you.

You will have a complete comprehension of how to terminate your Audible membership and confidently investigate alternative choices by the time you reach the conclusion of this book. In order to ensure that your experience with audiobooks continues to be pleasurable and satisfying, you will be armed with the knowledge necessary to make choices based on accurate information. You have the flexibility to explore, discover, and appreciate new tales and information on your own terms, and here is your guide to navigating the world of audiobooks beyond Audible. Your guide is here.

Chapter 1
What Is Audible?

Audible, an industry leader in the audiobook sector, is well-known for its huge collection and user-friendly features. It has established itself as a leading platform in the industry. First, let's take a look at the most important aspects of Audible, including its essential features and the advantages of its subscription service, so that you can completely realize why you could have selected Audible and understand what you might be leaving behind.

Key Features

Extensive collection of books

In order to satisfy the preferences of each and every listener, Audible provides one of the most extensive collections of audiobooks in the world. These audiobooks cover a wide variety of genres and categories. Audible's library is one of its most enticing aspects because of the sheer magnitude of its collection. Whether you are a lover of engrossing thrillers that keep you on the edge of your seat, uplifting romances that make you believe in love, or instructive biographies that provide deep insights into the lives of interesting people, Audible offers everything you could ever want to read.

Self-help books are available in a wide variety on Audible, catering to those who are interested in bettering themselves. These books cover a wide range of themes, including productivity, mental health, personal finance, and more. Additionally, there is an abundance of educational material, including audiobooks on topics like physics, history, and even language acquisition. With such a large selection of options, it is quite possible that you will be able to discover something that satisfies your preferences, regardless of the need or interest you have.

There is a large range of children's audiobooks available on Audible, in addition to the adult audiobooks that are available. These include both traditional fairy tales and contemporary works of fiction for young adults, making it a service that is suitable for families. With such a wide selection, it is possible for both parents and children to discover information that is pleasant, which helps to cultivate a love of reading and learning at a young age.

On top of that, Audible regularly refreshes its catalog by adding new releases as well as titles that are unique to the service. This ensures that customers get access to the most recent publications as soon as they are released to the public, therefore maintaining a listening experience that is both contemporary and new. The huge library is a big lure for people who value having a wide variety of selections available to them at their fingertips.

Audio of the Highest Quality
It is rare to find better audio quality than that of Audible. Professional narrators who are either experienced actors or the authors themselves narrate the audiobooks. These narrators provide

performances that are not only captivating but also emotionally moving. In order to make the experience of listening to a narrative more enjoyable, these narrators bring the characters to life by using various voices and a range of emotions.

Additionally, the production quality of Audible audiobooks is of the highest possible standard. High-quality sound engineering is used in the production of several titles, which guarantees that the audio will be clear and full of depth. Listeners are able to completely immerse themselves in the narrative without being distracted by bad sound quality or inconsistencies because to the attention to detail that has been paid to everything.

Audible takes the audiobook experience to the next level by including sound effects and music in some collections of audiobooks. These features have the potential to offer an additional degree of immersion, turning the listening experience into something more comparable to a radio play than a straightforward reading of a book or chapter. The use of ambient noises, which may heighten the tension and excitement of a story, is especially beneficial for genres such as horror.

In addition, the high-quality audio output makes listening for extended periods of time interesting. Whether you are listening to it throughout a lengthy commute, while you are working out, or while you are doing chores around the house, the higher audio quality guarantees that the experience will stay enjoyable and interesting for the whole of the listening experience.

Simple and Easy-to-Use Interface

The app that Audible offers is developed with the user's convenience and accessibility in mind, making it possible for listeners to have an experience that is both smooth and pleasurable. The application is accessible on a variety of platforms, including iOS, Android, and Windows, giving you the ability to listen to your audiobooks in a variety of settings using a variety of different methods.

When using the Audible app, navigating through it is a simple and uncomplicated process. The user interface is uncluttered and well-organized, which makes it simple to navigate the enormous library, search for particular titles, and maintain your own personal audiobook collection. With features such as bookmarking, you are able to instantly mark and return to key sections in an audiobook. This is especially helpful when you want to revisit favorite passages or while you are writing an academic paper.

It is a useful tool for both students and professionals since it has a note-taking capability that allows listeners to write down their ideas or crucial points while they are listening to the presentation. There is also a sleep timer function that enables you to set a timer for how long you want the audiobook to play. This helps you to fall asleep without having to worry about losing your position in the book. Anyone who enjoys listening to audiobooks as a method to relax before going to bed will find this to be an excellent option.

It is also possible to customize the settings for the font size and background color in the text display inside the Audible app, which allows it to accommodate a variety of visual tastes and requirements. It is now much simpler for everybody, regardless of their level of technological expertise, to enjoy listening to audiobooks thanks to these intelligent design aspects, which improve the entire user experience.

The Voice Whispersync System

In addition to being one of Audible's most notable features, Whispersync for Voice is a one-of-a-kind invention that allows you to synchronize the progress of your audiobook with your Kindle eBook. This function enables you to move between reading and listening without losing your position, providing you with a reading experience that is both flexible and integrated.

Take, for example, the scenario in which you begin reading an eBook on your Kindle while you are at home and then switch to listening to the audiobook version while you are traveling. You will be able to take up precisely where you left off since Whispersync will automatically update your progress. If you are a busy person who enjoys reading books in a variety of formats depending on what you are doing, this function is very helpful for you.

The use of Whispersync for voice is likewise advantageous for those who take pleasure in rereading passages or who have a need to examine certain chapters of a book. For the purpose of learning or conducting an in-depth examination of the content, the ability to quickly switch between text and audio is a useful feature. This synchronization of formats improves the whole of the reading experience by making it more flexible and adaptable to a variety of circumstances.

Personalized Recommendations and suggestions

A strong tool that makes recommendations that are tailored to your listening habits, the recommendation engine on Audible is a valuable tool. Audible is able to provide recommendations for new audiobooks that are suitable for your preferences and interests by evaluating your prior purchases, reviews, and listening history. Users are able to learn about new authors and genres that they would not have otherwise explored thanks to this customized touch.

As you continue to connect with the platform, the recommendation algorithm will continue to learn and improve over time, making it more accurate as it does so. Consequently, the quality of the suggestions will improve in proportion to the amount of time you spend using Audible. Using this feature, not only will your listening experience be improved, but it will also save you time by providing you with a selection of audiobooks that are likely to be of interest to you.

In addition, Audible provides curated lists and collections that are based on popular genres, topics, and trends that are currently occurring.

Discovering new audiobooks and keeping up with the latest trends in the industry may be accomplished with the help of these curated lists. Audible's tailored suggestions make the process of discovery more pleasurable and efficient, regardless of whether you are seeking the most recent hits, undiscovered treasures, or recommendations that are specialized to a certain genre.

Listening in Offline Mode

Through the use of Audible, you are able to ensure that you always have access to your preferred titles, regardless of whether or not you have an online connection. This is accomplished by downloading your audiobooks and listening to them offline. People who have lengthy commutes, who travel often, or who reside in places where internet connectivity is intermittent may find this function to be very helpful.

Listening to audiobooks offline is a simple process that may be downloaded. The titles that you wish to download are stored to your device once you have selected them. This guarantees that you can listen to your audiobooks whenever and wherever you want, without having to worry about data usage or network issues.

People who like listening to audiobooks while participating in activities that require them to be away from a solid internet connection, such as going on lengthy road trips, hiking, or camping, may also benefit from offline listening. Your pleasure is always within reach thanks to the offline listening function of Audible, which provides a listening experience that is smooth and uninterrupted.

Adjustable Playback Speed

Adjusting the playing speed of your audiobooks is something that Audible gives you the ability to do, giving you more control over your listening experience. Having the ability to adjust the tempo to suit your own preferences or to accommodate certain circumstances is a really helpful tool.

It is possible to boost the playback speed in order to speed up the process of getting through the information. This is an excellent option for reading novels that you are already acquainted with or for reading thrillers that move swiftly. In contrast, you may slow down the narrator's natural pace if you want to appreciate a narrative that is exceptionally fascinating or if you believe that the natural speed of the narrator is too quick.

Educational and professional audiobooks both benefit from having the ability to adjust the playing speed. When it comes to understanding and the ability to remember complicated material, slowing down the narration may be beneficial, while speeding it up might be helpful for review sessions. Because of this versatility, you will be able to completely personalize your audiobook experience to meet your specific listening requirements and preferences.

Subscription Benefits

Monthly Credits

This monthly credit system is one of the fundamental components that underpins Audible's subscription. This concept is intended to provide subscribers with both freedom and value in their purchasing decisions. Depending on the membership plan you select, you will receive a specific number of credits each month. Regardless of the standard price of the book, these credits may be redeemed for any audiobook that is available in Audible's vast collection. It is possible to have access to even the most costly titles without incurring any additional costs beyond the membership amount that you pay.

For those who are interested in purchasing high-priced, recently published publications or blockbusters that would otherwise be out of their financial grasp, the credit system is very helpful. This allows you to discover a large assortment of genres and authors without having to worry about the cost of each individual book. You can do this with the certainty that your monthly credit will cover the cost of the books. This technique makes it possible for more people to have access to premium audiobooks, which means that you may enjoy a wide range of material without breaking the bank.

Furthermore, if you do not utilize all of your credits in a certain month, they will often roll over to the next month. This provides you with the freedom to accrue credits and spend them when you uncover titles that you are really enthusiastic about. For example, if you have a particularly hectic month in which you don't have time to listen to as many books, this function will guarantee that the value of your membership continues to be preserved.

Member Discounts
In addition to the monthly credits, users of Audible get considerable savings on the purchase of extra audiobooks. If you want to increase your collection, you can do so for a fraction of the standard cost by taking advantage of this offer, which is applicable

to any audiobook in Audible's catalog. It doesn't matter whether you're wanting to buy an additional book for an upcoming vacation or if you just can't wait for your next credit; these reductions make it more reasonable to access more titles.

There is a good chance that the reductions will be large, with some being as much as thirty percent off the standard price. There are times when Audible offers special specials or deals that are only available to subscribers, and this advantage might be very enticing during such times. You will have the option to purchase books at a cheaper price compared to non-members when you take advantage of these member-only specials, which typically offer popular titles and new releases.

Member discounts often apply to various forms of audio material that are accessible on Audible, such as podcasts and original series, in addition to podcasts and audiobooks. Your membership will be even more useful as a result of this since it will include a wider range of material that you can enjoy at a lower cost.

Access to Audible Originals

A one-of-a-kind service that is only accessible to Audible members, Audible Originals are a remarkable product. Audible is responsible for producing audiobooks and other forms of audio entertainment, and it often includes works by well-known writers, dramatizations, and unique programs that are not available anywhere else. In addition to fiction, non-fiction, and humor, Audible Originals span a broad variety of other genres and formats as well.

In addition to having access to these unique titles, your membership grants you access to them as a subscriber. This means that you will have the opportunity to experience material that is both original and cutting-edge, which is not offered by any other audiobook service. For the purpose of delivering an immersive listening experience, Audible Originals often contain high-quality productions that include professional narration, sound effects, and music.

This exclusive material provides you with access to a handpicked collection of one-of-a-kind audiobooks and series, which is a considerable addition to the value of your membership. It doesn't matter whether you're searching for something fresh and unique or if you're trying to find works by your favorite writers; Audible Originals provide a listening experience that is both rich and diversified.

Free Audiobook Exchanges

Audible's hassle-free exchange policy is one of the most notable advantages of having a membership to the service. If you buy an audiobook and discover that it does not live up to your expectations, you have the option to quickly return or exchange it within the first year after purchase. This strategy guarantees that you are always happy with your library and that you are able to discover new titles without the fear of being forced to read a book that you do not love.

An easy and user-friendly exchange procedure is provided. Using the Audible website or app, you can easily initiate a refund or exchange with only a few clicks of the mouse. Because it enables a risk-free study of Audible's enormous collection, this function is especially helpful for those who may be experimenting with new genres or writers who are not acquainted with them.

If you are able to trade audiobooks, it makes you feel more confident in trying out new material because you are aware that you have the capacity to make adjustments if a specific title does not connect with you. The total value of the membership is increased as a result of this customer-friendly approach.

Exclusive Sales and Promotions
Audible regularly provides its members with access to special deals and promotions that are

only available to them, which results in extra possibilities to acquire audiobooks at significant discounts. As a result of the fact that these bargains often contain popular titles, bestsellers, and new releases, this is a perfect opportunity to add to your collection without paying a significant amount of money.

On occasion, sales events that are exclusive to members may provide substantial discounts, perhaps reaching up to fifty percent or even more. Purchase-one-get-one-free discounts, bundle offers, and seasonal specials are some of the other types of promotions that Audible provides on a regular basis. In addition to providing members with additional value, these promotions also provide you the opportunity to take advantage of limited-time discounts and unique price options.

Not only do these unique discounts and promotions make it more inexpensive to develop a wide and comprehensive audiobook collection, but they also create a feeling of belonging to a privileged group of individuals who have access to exceptional bargains and offers.

Audible Plus Catalog

As part of the Audible Plus membership package, users get unrestricted access to a variety of audiobooks, podcasts, and Audible Originals that are always being updated. Through the inclusion of this library in the subscription, you will be able to listen to an unlimited number of titles without depleting your monthly credits. Active listeners who take in a substantial amount of audio material will find this to be a considerable advantage.

From classic literature to modern fiction, self-help, humor, and a wide variety of other genres and formats, the library of Audible Plus covers a wide variety of titles. The feature that allows for limitless listening gives you the opportunity to discover new authors and genres without having to worry about incurring extra charges or using up your credit.

Anyone who enjoys binge-listening to programs or who wants to taste a broad range of material will find this tier of the subscription to be especially intriguing. It makes it possible to enjoy a wide variety of audio entertainment in a manner that is both flexible and economical.

Immersive Audio Experiences
In order to provide a more cinematic listening experience, several audiobooks in Audible's collection have been developed with immersive soundscapes and multi-voice performances. In order to deliver an audio experience that goes beyond the basic act of reading a book, these productions make use of the platform that Audible provides.

In order to create a rich and interesting aural environment, immersive audio experiences often consist of sound effects, music, and many narrators that provide the voices of various characters. In the realms of fantasy, science fiction, and thrillers, where atmospheric sound design has the potential to enhance the plot, this sort of production is especially successful.

By making a decent tale into an extraordinary one, these high-quality productions have the potential to make the listening experience more delightful and memorable for the listener. The fact that Audible is dedicated to developing material of this kind distinguishes it from other audiobook services, allowing it to provide members with listening experiences that are both distinctive and of great value.

Easy Cancellation

It is possible to cancel your membership to Audible at any moment without incurring any additional costs or going through any onerous procedures since the subscription model is meant to be flexible and user-friendly. It is simple to terminate your subscription with Audible using either the mobile app or the website if you come to the conclusion that the service no longer fulfills your requirements.

In addition, the cancellation procedure is simple and open to public scrutiny. To guarantee that you are able to finish the procedure quickly and without any problem, Audible offers instructions that are easy to understand. People who wish to manage their subscriptions without feeling like they are being locked in or punished will find this freedom to be a great advantage.

Your ability to regulate your membership and ensure that you only pay for the service when it satisfies your requirements and preferences is reflected in Audible's customer-centric approach, which is reflected in the company's simple cancellation policy. Audible's membership is a risk-free alternative for experiencing the world of audiobooks because of its flexibility, which contributes to the overall attractiveness of the service.

Chapter 2

Reasons to Cancel Audible

Despite the fact that Audible provides a multitude of advantages, there are factors that might lead some customers to contemplate terminating their membership. The majority of the time, these causes may be broken down into two primary categories: everyday problems with the service and shifting preferences on an individual level.

Common Issues with Audible

1. Cost Concerns

The cost of an Audible membership is a crucial consideration that lots of users consider when deciding whether or not to discontinue their subscription. There is a possibility that the monthly charge and the possible additional expenditures for buying more credits or audiobooks might pile up over time, despite the fact that the subscription plans offered by Audible provide a fair value for ardent listeners. It is possible that consumers who are on a limited budget or who are attempting to reduce costs that are not essential would find this fee to be bothersome. It is possible that the expense of keeping an Audible membership may seem unreasonable, especially in the event that consumers discover that they do not make as much use of the service as they had expected.

2. Underutilization

Audible subscriptions are often underutilized because of the demands that life places on its users. Even if one has the best of intentions, it is possible that they will not have enough time to listen to audiobooks on a consistent basis due to their hectic schedules and conflicting responsibilities. When customers find that they are not making use of their monthly credits, which accrue without being redeemed, this underutilization has the potential to become quite irritating. In spite of the fact that Audible permits credits to be carried over, there is a limit on the total number of credits that may be accumulated. When consumers do not make continuous use of their credits, they may have a feeling of discontent with the service since they may believe that they are squandering resources.

3. Technical Difficulties

Audible is known for having an intuitive user interface; nonetheless, there are some customers who have technical issues that interfere with their listening experience. Problems that have the potential to be irritating and disruptive include app crashes, sluggish download rates, and difficulties with the playing of audiobooks. If users encounter these technological issues on a regular basis, it may lead to a decrease in utilization and a decrease in their overall happiness with the service. It is possible that users may get dissatisfied with the perceived lack of dependability and look for other platforms that have technology that operates more smoothly.

4. Content Availability

There are times when certain titles or genres that customers are interested in may not be accessible on Audible, despite the fact that the service claims huge libraries. Especially for users who have specialized interests or who are looking for the most recent releases in their favored genres, this constraint in material availability might be a considerable disadvantage. Users may perceive a sense of limitation and look for alternatives that provide a wider variety of audiobooks to pick from if Audible is unable to supply the material that they demand or if there are delays in the creation of new releases.

5. Customer Service Issues

It is possible for customers to have varying experiences with customer care, and it is possible that some users may have difficulty resolving problems or obtaining help from Audible's customer service staff. Examples of bad customer service, sluggish response times, or remedies to issues that are not sufficient may all contribute to a decrease in the level of happiness that users have with the entire experience. The users who have the impression that their complaints are not appropriately handled may experience feelings of frustration and disillusionment, which may lead them to investigate other audiobook platforms that provide customer care that is more responsive and helpful.

6. Audible's Exchange Policy

Although the exchange policy of Audible is generally considered to be user-friendly, there are some users who may feel the constraints of the policy to be limiting. For instance, users who have previously traded many audiobooks can discover that they are unable to trade another audiobook that they believe to be unacceptable. It is possible for people to get frustrated as a result of this limitation, particularly if they believe that they are not getting value for their money. It is possible that users will be dissuaded from continuing their subscription if they believe that the exchange policy does not provide sufficient flexibility. This is especially true if they believe that their requirements and preferences are not effectively satisfied.

Changing Preferences and Alternative Options

1. Shift in Listening Habits

An individual's tastes and habits are dynamic and might change throughout the course of their lifetime. As you get more interested in other types of media, you could discover that your interest in audiobooks tends to decrease. When you listen to podcasts, listen to music, or read physical books, for instance, you can find that you have a renewed enthusiasm for those media. Maintaining an Audible membership may no longer be in line with your ever-changing interests and preferences if you find that your interest in listening to audiobooks increases.

2. Exploring Other Formats

Beyond audiobooks, there is a wealth of other alternatives available to users since the landscape of media use is constantly shifting. You may want to investigate alternate formats, such as eBooks or physical books, that provide a better fit for your lifestyle or interests as technology continues to progress. As opposed to audiobooks, you could find that the physical feel of having a book in your hands or the ease of accessing eBooks on digital devices is more appealing to you. Getting familiar with these many formats gives you the opportunity to broaden your reading experience and discover the format that caters to your tastes the most effectively.

3. Alternative Services
Alternate services that cater to a wide variety of interests and requirements have emerged as a result of the considerable increase that the audiobook industry has undergone. Some examples of platforms that provide competitive pricing, innovative features, and extensive content libraries are Scribd, Google Play Books, and public library applications like Libby. It is possible that these alternatives provide feasible possibilities that are more in line with the limits of your budget or that give unique material that is relevant to your interests. You will be able to find new platforms that are more successful in meeting your

audiobook demands if you experiment with these alternative providers.

4. Access to Free Content

People who are interested in saving money have an appealing option in the shape of a multitude of free audio material that is accessible across a variety of platforms. The majority of the time, public libraries provide free audiobook rentals via services such as OverDrive or Libby. These services enable access to a huge variety of titles without the expense that is associated with a membership. In addition, websites such as YouTube and certain podcasts provide free access to a wide variety of audio information, which includes listening to novels, lectures, and stories. By using these free resources, you are able to take pleasure in listening to audio material without having to subscribe to a service that requires a financial commitment.

5. Specific Needs or Interests

It's possible that your interests and requirements may change over time, which could cause you to look for specialized material that might not be easily accessible on Audible. For instance, if you have a strong interest in specialized subjects, educational courses, or language acquisition, you may be able to locate specialized platforms that are better suited to cater to your interests specifically. Offering individualized content that is more closely aligned with your interests, specialized services provide an experience that is both more fulfilling and more concentrated. Exploring these specialist platforms gives you the opportunity to get more in-depth information on subjects that are of specific interest to you and to broaden your knowledge in areas that are important to you.

6. Desire for a Different User Experience
The desire to have a different user experience may sometimes be the driving force behind the choice to investigate other platforms or to terminate your membership to Audible. It's possible that other audiobook providers offer features or interfaces that are more closely aligned with your tastes. For example, they could provide smooth interaction with other devices, easy navigation, or better customer support. You may select a platform that

offers a user experience that resonates with you by exploring a variety of platforms. This will help you to enjoy audiobooks more consistently as a result.

To summarize, despite the fact that Audible provides a comprehensive audiobook service, users may be compelled to investigate other platforms or terminate their memberships due to the fact that their tastes are always shifting and there are other choices available. Understanding these factors enables you to make educated judgments about the amount of audiobooks you consume, whether it is because of evolving habits, the desire to explore various forms, or unique content requirements.

Chapter 3
Canceling Your Audible Subscription

With the Audible website or mobile app, you may easily cancel your membership to Audible. This is a simple and straightforward procedure. To cancel your membership, please follow these detailed steps, step by step:

Step-by-Step Instructions:

1. Log In:

a. Visit the Audible Website or Open the Audible Mobile App:

- Begin by accessing the Audible platform through either the Audible website on your computer or by opening the Audible mobile app on your smartphone or tablet.

- If using the website, launch your preferred web browser and navigate to the Audible homepage. Alternatively, locate the Audible app icon on your mobile device's home screen or app drawer and tap to open it.

b. Log In to Your Audible Account:

- Once you've accessed the Audible platform, proceed to log in to your Audible account using the credentials associated with your account.

- Enter your username or email address, and password in the designated fields provided on the login screen.

2. Navigate to Account Details:

a. Locate account details or settings:

- After successfully logging in, navigate to your account details or settings page within the Audible platform.

- On the website, this option is typically accessible by clicking on your profile name or picture, which may be located in the upper right corner of the screen. A dropdown menu should appear, displaying various account-related options, including "Account Details" or "Settings."

- In the Audible mobile app, access your account details by tapping on the menu icon (often represented by three horizontal lines or a profile picture) located in the top-left or top-right corner of the screen. Look for an option labeled "Account Settings" or similar.

3. Subscription Settings:

a. Locate Subscription Settings or Membership Details:
- Within your account settings or details page, locate the section specifically dedicated to subscription settings or membership details.
- This section may be labeled "Membership" or "Subscription" and is typically found within the broader account settings menu.

b. Look for the cancellation option:
- Once you've accessed the subscription settings or membership details, scan the options available for any feature related to canceling or ending your subscription.
- Audible may present you with various options, such as pausing your membership, downgrading to a different plan, or outright canceling your subscription. Focus on identifying the specific cancellation option.

4. Cancellation Option:

a. Click on the option to cancel:

- Upon locating the cancellation option, click or tap on it to initiate the cancellation process.

- Depending on Audible's interface and current promotions, you may encounter additional options or incentives, such as pausing your membership temporarily instead of canceling it outright.

b. Choose the cancellation option:

- If presented with multiple choices, ensure to select the option that explicitly states "Cancel Membership" or a similar wording to proceed with canceling your Audible subscription.

5. Confirmation Prompt:

a. Review the confirmation information:

- After selecting the cancellation option, Audible will likely present you with a confirmation prompt detailing the consequences of canceling your subscription.

- Take the time to carefully read through the information provided to ensure you understand any implications or changes to your account.

6. Follow the confirmation steps:

a. Follow any additional steps or prompts:

- Depending on Audible cancellation process, you may be required to follow additional steps or prompts to complete the cancellation process.

- This could include confirming your decision again, providing feedback on why you're canceling your subscription (which is optional but can help Audible improve its service), or answering a brief survey.

7. Confirmation email:

a. Check your email inbox:

- After successfully completing the cancellation process, Audible should send you a confirmation email to the email address associated with your account.

- Check your email inbox, including any spam or junk folderthat youhat youo locate the confirmation email from Audible.

- Ensure to double-check your email settings to ensure that emails from Audible are not being filtered out or marked as spam.

b. Verify the receipt of confirmation:

- Open the confirmation email from Audible and verify that it confirms the cancellation of your subscription.

- The email should provide confirmation details, such as the date of cancellation and any relevant account changes.

Troubleshooting Tips:

Unable to Find Cancellation Option:

a. Utilize search functionality:

- Try using the platform's search feature if you're having trouble finding the option to cancel your subscription within your account settings.

- Use keywords such as "membership," "subscription," or "billing" to narrow down the search results and locate the relevant cancellation option.

   b. Explore Different Menu Sections:
   - Audible's platform may organize account settings into multiple sections or menus. Explore different areas, such as "Billing," "Account Management," or "Membership Details," to locate the cancellation option.
   - Don't overlook submenus or dropdown lists within each section, as the cancellation option may be nested within these menus.

Check membership status:

   a. Access Account Information:
   - Before attempting to cancel your Audible subscription, verify that your membership is currently active and not already canceled or expired.

- Access your account information or membership details to confirm the status of your Audible subscription.

b. Look for a renewal date:

- Check the renewal date associated with your Audible membership to ensure that it hasn't lapsed or been terminated.
- If your membership has already been canceled or expired, you may not see the option to cancel again, as there would be no active subscription to cancel.

Contact Customer Support:

a. Access Customer Support Options:

- If you encounter any issues or difficulties during the cancellation process, don't hesitate to reach out to Audible's customer support for assistance.
- Access the customer support options provided by Audible, which may include live chat, email support, or a dedicated help center.

b. Provide Details of Issue:

- When contacting customer support, provide specific details regarding the issue you're experiencing with canceling your Audible subscription.

- Include any error messages or screenshots, if applicable, to help expedite the resolution process.

Review Terms and Conditions:

a. Access Audible's Terms and Conditions:

- Before proceeding with the cancellation of your Audible subscription, take the time to review Audible's terms and conditions.

- Pay particular attention to sections related to refunds, credits, and access to purchased content after cancellation to understand any potential implications.

b. Clarify refund policies:

- Familiarize yourself with Audible's refund policies, especially regarding any unused credits or remaining subscription periods.

- Understand the timeframe and eligibility criteria for requesting refunds or credits, if applicable.

Consider pausing membership.

a. Explore Temporary Options:

- If you're unsure about permanently canceling your Audible subscription, consider exploring temporary alternatives, such as pausing your membership.

- Pausing your membership allows you to temporarily suspend your subscription without losing access to your account or accumulated credits.

b. Evaluate the duration:

- Evaluate the duration for which you intend to pause your Audible membership and ensure that it aligns with your needs and preferences.

- Keep in mind any potential limitations or restrictions associated with pausing your membership, such as the maximum duration allowed.

Double-check billing information:

a. Verify payment method:

- Before proceeding with the cancellation process, double-check the billing information associated with your Audible account.

- Ensure that your credit card details or chosen payment method are up-to-date and valid to prevent any issues with canceling your subscription.

b. Update billing information if necessary:

- If your billing information is outdated or incorrect, update it accordingly within your Audible account settings before attempting to cancel your subscription.

- Incorrect billing information may prevent you from successfully completing the cancellation process.billing

By following these expanded troubleshooting tips, you can address potential obstacles and navigate the cancellation process with confidence. If you encounter any difficulties, don't hesitate to reach out to Audible's customer support for further assistance and guidance.

Chapter 4
Addressing Attachment When Cancelling Audible

Recognize emotional attachment:

Understanding the Significance:
If you have been a dedicated member to Audible for a considerable amount of time or have amassed a sizeable collection of audiobooks, it is not uncommon to develop a profound emotional connection with the service over the course of time. Always keep in mind the sentimental worth and emotional investment that is associated with your Audible membership and collection.

Personal Connection to Audiobooks:
When used as a form of entertainment, audiobooks often become more than simply a source of amusement; they may become companions during commutes, exercises, or alone. Give some thought to the personal relevance of certain audiobooks in

your collection, as well as the memories or feelings that they create with you.

Community and Connection:
Many users find that Audible provides them with more than just access to audiobooks; it also gives them a feeling of belonging to a community of other listeners who have interests and passions that are similar to their own. Consider the relationships you've established via the use of Audible, whether it's by getting together with friends to talk about your favorite books or through taking part in online discussion groups and book clubs.

Reflect on Reasons for Attachment:

Exploring Motivations:
Identify the fundamental causes for your relationship to your Audible membership by taking some time to reflect on yourself and identifying the reasons. What is it about having the ability to listen to audiobooks whenever and wherever you

want? What about the extensive range of titles that cover a variety of genres? Or maybe it's the sensation of being a part of a wider community of people who are passionate about books.

Emotional Fulfillment:
Take into consideration the ways in which your Audible membership satisfies your cognitive and emotional demands, such as relaxation, escape, and intellectual stimulation. Take some time to think about the functions that audiobooks fulfill in your daily routine and the ways in which they contribute to your general pleasure and sense of well-being.

Nostalgia and Memories:
It's possible that some audiobooks have a nostalgic value due to the fact that they bring back recollections of key life events, treasured experiences, or moments of personal development. Investigate the sense of emotional connection that you have developed with certain audiobooks, as well as the ways in which these books have influenced your experiences and your attitude.

Embrace change and Growth:

Acceptance of Transition:

It is normal to outgrow some habits, preferences, or commitments, and it is important to acknowledge that change is an unavoidable aspect of life. Accept the possibility that canceling your Audible membership might serve as a catalyst for your own personal development and the introduction of new experiences.

Opportunity for Exploration:

If you decide to cancel your Audible membership, you should look at it as a chance to discover new hobbies, find other audiobook services, or get back in touch with other kinds of media. Allow yourself the opportunity to extend your horizons and expand your literary interests by embracing the flexibility to explore various audiobook platforms and genres.

Self-Reflection and Adaptation:

Seize the chance to engage in self-reflection and adaptation during this moment of transformation. Consider the ways in which your tastes and requirements for audiobooks have changed over the course of time, as well as the ways in which they may continue to change in the future. Adopt a positive attitude toward the process of self-discovery and adaptation, keeping in mind that your interests and priorities may change throughout time, which may result in experiences that are both fresh and satisfying.

Conclusion

The choice to terminate your membership to Audible is impacted by a wide range of circumstances, both physiological and psychological. It is possible to cancel for a variety of personal and different reasons, including worries about cost, underutilization, technological difficulties, available material, and problems with customer support. Changing preferences, such as a change in listening habits, the desire to explore other formats, the availability of alternative services, access to free material, and unique requirements or interests, all contribute to the decision-making process. One example of a changing preference is the desire to explore different formats.

Logging into your account, going to the settings for your subscription, choosing the cancellation option, and then following the prompts to confirm your choice are the steps that are involved in the process of canceling your Audible membership. This procedure is basic in terms of the practical processes. Some of the troubleshooting tips that are available to you in the event that you experience any difficulties include the following: making use of the search functions within the account settings; verifying the status of your membership; contacting customer support; reviewing the terms and conditions; considering pausing your membership; and ensuring that your billing information is up to date.

If you have any kind of emotional link to Audible, it is essential to acknowledge and deal with it. Consider the reasons for your relationship to your audiobook collection, acknowledge the sentimental significance and emotional investment that it has, and be open to the possibility of personal development and change. Providing yourself with reassurance and reaching out to others for support are also additional ways to make the shift easier.

At the end of the day, the objective is to design a listening and reading experience that is congruent with your way of life and contributes to your wellness as a whole. Trust that you are making the right decision for yourself at this point in your journey, regardless of whether you choose to continue using Audible, switch to a new service, or take a vacation from purchasing audiobooks entirely.

If you found this book helpful, we would be deeply grateful if you could take a moment to leave a positive and honest review. Your feedback is incredibly important.

Warmest regards,
BlazeTech

Made in the USA
Monee, IL
07 September 2025